JOUSTING FROM THE BACK OF A MULE

JOUSTING FROM THE BACK OF A MULE

POEMS

BY

TED ARCHER POPE

REDHAWK
PUBLICATIONS

Published by Redhawk Publications

2550 US Hwy 70 SE

Hickory, NC 28602

REDHAWK PUBLICATIONS

Robert Canipe, Publisher and Editor-in-Chief

Tim Peeler, Editor

Patty Thompson, Project and Permissions Coordinator

Originally published by Third Lung Press © 2004

Cover Line Art by Eric C. Harrison

ISBN: 978-1-952485-27-5

TABLE OF CONTENTS

THIS WEEKS SPECIA
9 PCS CHICKEN
ONLY $14 00
FRIE ROLLS $16 85

JOUSTING FROM THE BACK OF A MULE

I am jousting from the back of a mule.

Oh timeless, mother Isis.

Grant me yet another hour

to perfect the walk

I will walk to the grave.

Paint the mask I will wear in death.

Jesus, Isis, Osiris, Buddha.

Someday some artist will paint me.

Embarrassed for me upon my mule,

he will paint me instead upon a White Stallion,

a steed of swift air

and green muscle.

UNTITLED

By the time you have learned the concept of innocence,

yours will be gone

lost

somewhere in transit

the roads all narrow,

all long

each searching for his own way

my dream has turned

more like the ancient

to seek out the original face.

Rise up walk in through the mountains

tomorrow down to the sea,

but the place to which I am truly traveling,

the hidden temple in me.

Know that when I get there

I will fall down and worship something

that is not me at all;

the illusions of this world will crumble,

the lies all topple and fall,

so if it's truth from which we are hiding,

join hands; there is no need to scream.

We may yet find ourselves

well within the spell of the dream.

No, I do not mean sleeping;

forever awake have you been,

just a point beyond all that confusion out there

where our original faces meet.

And I used to be a cruel character,

Act III, second scene,

but I have closed the book on that paragraph,

for the play is no longer of me.

It is the tapestry of the universe

and the threads weave a simple theme

and converge at a point beyond all the confusion

where our Original Faces meet.

WORMWOOD

The Japan Sea,

the Ukraine,

burial grounds of Russian

poisons of war and peace,

viral infections,

chemical weapons

and nuclear wastes,

tombs of secret

super-soldiers

and their victims

a hundred meters below

the perma-frost

lying in heaps,

submarines and mammoth bones

waiting for a second coming,

a day of judgment,

an invasion,

fleet of great mother ships

arriving with a cure for death

at "a certain hour."

strange

now

forests, lakes, tundras,

and cold deeps,

haunted by dark, spirits foul

with the shit of our paranoia,

running from our mouths and ears

because we are not watchful,

because we are not valiant.

LIKE FALLING INTO YOUR ARMS

Your face is too big

or else we're too close.

You want what we all want.

Start with loneliness, frustration,

or love,

divine diamonds of the heart's mind

they shine,

the eyes set way back

under the war helmet

of one of Hannibal's soldiers

crossing the Alps at night

on the back of his elephant,

like moving into your world,

like falling into your arms.

JOHNNY APPLESEED, AMERICAN DIONYSIUS

Remember him when the cider hits your lips,

when the sweetness cracks its whip,

so red, so delicious.

Spot it with a hawk eye. Sell it to corporate America,

wrapped in barbed wire. Build a cage around it.

Dedicate a chant.

Oh, I been alone. I been dethroned. I walked through

the poppies in the fields. I have been taken up into

outer space.

And even when the aliens dissected me,

they could not get this mask off my face,

and so

they set me back down

into your gothic garden

where witches ride broomstick dildoes,

chanting tripping spells.

I hurry past them

into the gymnasium

where I am instructed in the art of war

by some jaded Obi Wan.

The little man

with the yellow hat

carrying a scroll that is sealed with wax.

The man in black

with the jug of wine.

Is it sour? Is it divine?

the girl in blue with the silver flute;

her melody flies true and straight,

the courtesan with the raven hair.

All the young guards want to place their flowers there.

I been known myself to become a pain in the ass.

I been known to travel to the gates of hell and come back,

but I never truly feel free

unless I am good and drunk on the wine of eternity.

Keep me on your good side,

or I will stay on your bad.

Drag out your Victrola

old

slow and sad,

cause this here bad news could use

some music to back it up.

some music to back it up.

GREAT ASS

You got a great Ass!

Why don't ya use it to make some money?

Or else to end the tribal genocide in darkest Africa?

Why with an ass like that you could signal the aliens to

come right on down here.

They would be so pleased to meet us.

Why an ass like that could feed the starving masses.

You got a great Ass!

Why I bet you can shine a light

right out of your perfect Asshole

and warn the great oil tankers of treacherous rocks.

SEVEN HABITS OF HIGHLY ANNOYING PEOPLE

Goddamn Amelia Airhart was a sexy chica!

slender. sliver. silver. propeller.

Beautiful in the sun-like lover.

I gotta die.

Ohhh…how I hate it!

But in this meantime: the golden knife and fork

the cup of tin, the wooden spoon…

Where's my hat?

Forget the mother fucker.

Forget the mother fucker.

That is the mantra that will keep you sane,

Along with the Koran chuck it in the sea…become

Desireless…Desire must be overcome!

It's like red says stop while symbolizing speed.

In time your dick will get wet again,

and you will smile.

Sure you will.

I need a chariot with wheels of fire. All I got today

was another nail in my tire.

a thousand thieves of virginity,

inside the flames,

and outside?

the sea,

and in between you lie in fitful sleep.

The waves are eating up the beach

and beneath them…vampires, diseases,

home mortgages and black-hatted cowboys.

This sea is death.

Its glue is blood,

the bones they use to beat the drums.

I can hear them,

pounding…pounding…pounding…poundin

g…

all over the island,

as they pick up the clocks scattered in the vineyard.

YOUR HEAD IS FILLED WITH THRUSHES

Your head is filled with thrushes.

Your heart burns.

Night burns twilight from the chimney

hunting the prey.

It is the first night of summer.

You are living inside the moon,

The windows open.

You lie back

with a wine glass in your hand,

warm,

high,

calm.

CUNTS AND WITCHCRAFT

Cunts and witchcraft were the only things Grandpa

feared

as the family houseboat cruised up the Nile.

We all feared the River Pirates!

but Grandpa had his guns; the only thing that he feared

were

the witchcraft and the cunts.

We

were afraid in the dark.

Little brother cried to see the slit-eyed crocs

but Grandpa just laughed and lit up a smoke.

The only things he feared

were the witchcraft and the cunts.

Some undead bastards screamed at us from the shore.

Grandpa

Only leaned upon the houseboat rail lookin' bored.

We

all did the Shuffle

just like vampires

in the sun.

but Grandpa

he stayed cool in his big straw hat.

The only things he feared were

the witchcraft and the cunts.

Tom Waits, Tom Waits, Tom waits, tom Waits, tom
waiTS, tom wAits, tom waIts…

we have at last reached the event horizon

where tom waits' droppings may be used as hard currency.

That's right, folks.

Step up to witness as a white-gloved attendant stands by,

a sterling bowl nestled in his mitts ready and waiting for

tom to take a dump there.

Spectators stand by

mouths watering

dreaming

of all the health food they will buy,

vials of swans tongues, velvet cucumber extract, seed of

storm giants, elixirs made from flowers so red

that they must only be harvested while wearing a welder's

mask.

GO!

Soil yourself! Tom!

We're all waiting,

and it's less than 200 days till the Christ Mass.

We need gifts

we need gifts!

we need gifts!

we need gifts!

gold, frankincense, myrrh,

and a little fat turd for the Christ child's hand.

Tom is here

smelling like an animal dressed as a shepherd.

You'd think a guy like Tom'd go

For the wiseman-wise guy look,

but no.

from the shadows of his woolen cowl,

he leers across the manger at the new-little mother,

and growls in his low tones…

"so how you doin' tonight Mary darlin'?"

The stars overhead tinkle their twinkling ivories.

HAMMER

Have you seen the dead
their candied smiles
the flowers grow over?
Have you looked down into his eyes lately, baby?
seen the terrible way they hang all over you?
I believe he's got a great big power now, and big hunger
and one of these moonlit nights he's going to come right
down here and swallow everything we've ever known.
When I look out to the new horizon
when I look back at the seeds I've sown,
the sure true sick feeling of a history set in stone.
Maybe the lightning striking will show us all
what's been hiding in the dark.

What about your ideas and ideas? What have you got
now, baby, except dust in your hand to hold?
All those wise men have left you right here standing;
All of the wise ones have flown with the crow.
Maybe some lightning striking
would show us all what's hiding in the dark.
I myself
drifted in here like a nightmare.

I myself have downed in all my hopes and dreams,
and I've burned up and I've burned down and I've
burned and I've burned offerings
still
no voice
from anywhere
has ever guided me.

Lucifer, however, has been thrown down among you
like a hammer,
like some fiery stone,
like a Big-Man ablaze
with the white hot light of alcohol, perfume, and stars.
He rapes the earth, the air, the atom,
and Lucifer has raped all of the hearts
of all the people I've ever known.
Maybe the lightning striking
will show us what's been hiding in the dark.

When I look out on the horizon,
when I look back on the deeds that I've done,
I get that sure sick feeling,
the hammer,
my hands swinging.
Maybe the lightning striking
will show us ourselves in the dark.

BRIGHT CHILD

Where are you glowing?

radiating your eternal primal essence.

You've got me bright child.

You got me from the first time I saw you crawl across the open

floor that first time that I saw you walk upon fire you've got

me bright child holy child child of all my hope and reverence I

saw her coming down 4th St. again today and today would not

be like any other day oh no today I'm going to follow her to

see where she goes to get that glowing eternal primal essence

follow me if you can she knows I've got a little leather left

upon the soles of my shoes so I do I do follow her down in my

flat-footed gait to where she waits upon that glowing eternal

primal essence a smiling Japanese tea garden even this the

moon garden of the sun but none as clear and bright and pure
as her

take some tea says the man in the corner behind me I did not

know the corner was there I did not know the man was there
he

smiles and I bow I'll take anything anything that you've got

and he's gone away to get my tea the bright child girl where is

she she's there upon the low wall the cherry blossoms hanging

across her face like a veil. It is her wedding day.

JOHNNY CASH'S ASHES

Johnny Cash's ashes
keep them close at hand
in a jewel encrusted urn
behind the coffee on the pantry shelf
against the day that Arthur comes back
and we need the man in black
to play Merlin to the returned king,

but the countryside is growing smaller
can you feel
it's getting worse here every year
and I believe
we've all grown fa-fa-fa-fearless
now the final lesson is close at hand.

In country song # 1
I hauled you in and I hurt you bad
I know it must be hard to believe
coming from me but honeysuckle
that was then
and this here is now.

And I am smashed in the face with the poor quality

of the light in this here room tonight

in anger I tear the postcard note

what do you wanna write to him for now anyway?

in anger

I pull on my candy-coat and stroll out

Into the countryside again.

But the countryside is getting smaller

can you feel

it feels worse around here every year

and I believe

we've all grown

fa-fa-fa-fearless

the final lesson is now at hand.

100 years of winter is now at hand.

BONUS POEMS

MAYBE

Then that cat will stay out for the night

Yep that was pretty dumb he sang

staring into the scorched eye at the bottom of the pan

Pretty dumb

We learned to make chicken stock

We learned leaving well enough alone was a shower of sparks

We learned to press a poem so it could be discovered flat and dry

We learned the origin of Limousine was the hood of a carriage and the origin of the hood of the carriage had its origin in the hood of a shepherd or monk

we discovered the butterfly effect couldn't hold a candle to the mosquito effect and that a single candle had reunited all of feudal Japan

We learned that frying an egg on a hot stone would not cure menstrual cramps but wasn't a bad poultice for hunger

We discovered practical jokes

A kingpin had a mule swallow Coney Island and smuggle it into Dubai

Then the circus came to town and the big top the roustabouts put up covered the whole municipality so now the town was the circus and everyone was walking tightropes and taming lions and had eyebrows like cotton candy

When grandpa died of a broken heart they used a box of old love letters to set the corpse ablaze roasted marshmallows and made s'mores

I don't believe that kinda behavior is reprehensible rather say it's unproductive

Tonight we watched shadows more lively than a harem of dancers performing on the great carcass of a beached leviathan

we knew from the bubbles he'd died of the bends we'd learned that even these grand marine mammals must guard against surfacing w/ too much haste.

We learned so many things.

from **THE LAST EPIC**

when the alcohol

level

falls that far

you wake up to remember

exactly who you are

wild-eyed

tongue-tied

and twisted

from

waking up

out

in

the water spout

wandering home alone

taking the oath

vowing

never

to Ever

let Food come before Poetry again

vowing

never

to ever wait again

like the Father

waits

all his life

for the child

to achieve happiness

why their

every joy

may seem like an end

the final assurance that

none of this is worth a damn!

birds cry

the shore line

answers with the undertow

deep Neptune

dreams

for us

his children

that find

a leap of faith

we ourselves

cannot quite

make

peyote

heals me

like a satellite

transporting

each and every one of my

dreams

up and out

there

through

the Twilight

twilight where the sun is sinking into

the sea revealing

every star in the galaxy

six degrees is civil twilight

you are safe

chasing lightning bugs

in your backyard.

Twelve degrees is nautical twilight

A navigator drowning in the cold

glaring up at the stars that

should've guided him home.

Eighteen degrees astronomical twilight

the sun sinking below the

sea revealing each and every one

of the stars to me.

See that one

No, the one on the left.

That was you before you were born.

I am driving

through these emotions

like I am

driving through a storm.

UNCLE BURTON

1

at the viewing
waiting
for Uncle Burton's body suddenly
to sputter and lurch to life
the way his old tractor did
each spring

i know he is watching me
when i turn on the tool shed's bare-bulb
swinging by the ancient cord that disappears up
into the dark rafters of that cathedral of bent nails,
rust and kerosene

he is whispering in the bottomland
it is not just the wind in the pines
but him
sometimes i hear him walking in the cornfield
just a few rows in...
though i have never parted the stalks to look
i am wholly sure it is him.

2

Uncle Burton had found a lot of artifacts on his land

especially near the river

old catawba pottery sherds and arrowheads...

when we were children Uncle Burton would walk in the woods with my brother and me

he would tell us that he could hear the indians singing in the woods near the river...

that it wasn't just the water and the rocks... but voices.

that he was wholly sure it was the singing of the first people to live there

maybe a week before he died I was out at the farm and Uncle Burton brought up the voices...

He asked me if I remembered him telling me about those Indians singing...

Sure I did. My brother did too.

Well said Uncle Burton... they are still there but

if they build that god-damn high-way, won't nobody be able to hear em.

maybe not ever again.

3

the old place had been renovated

rewired

but the ghost was still there...

in the timbers

his voice a loose piece of tin

conversing with the westerly wind

i put the key in the tractor's ignition

but it is his hand turns it

reaching into the Oliver's old tool box

his arm reaches in too

helping me search out

a block of wood

a length of chain

4

It was a good thing Uncle Burton had died

a year ago happy

instead of seeing the bottom land dissected by the by-pass

the stream choked with debris

its special powers silenced by an oily film

the soccer fields replacing tobacco

the chemicals green the turf... runoff

into the groundwater so

they still get cancer those kids

their parents doing all that driving

used to be a night like this was filled with croakers and
lightning bugs

now it's nothing but brake lights and car horns

if man had been meant to drive, God would have made him with his middle finger eternally extended

It was a good thing Uncle Burton had died

a year ago happy

train engineers don't even blow their own whistles any more

sure it's safer

the computer never forgets

maybe all that safety will give us space to spin yarns like vibrant transcendent spiders

orbs of energy

or maybe we will just atrophy in a casing

that lacks sweet sap

nourishment

the power company

murdered the mammoth oak in the pasture

paved it over

I sold the last of the cows and became wholly convinced

Uncle Burton had died happy a year ago.

THE POETRY READING is survived by:

the poet.

the poet's family.

the poet's friends many of whom are also poets.

poets who aren't friends of the poet but who go to poetry readings with the unspoken expectation that the favor be returned.

young poets who pretend even to themselves that they saw sumthing inspiring so they don't have to face what a waste the evening was.

one of the poets in attendance claimed that the Poetry Reading could have been saved if they had moved it full speed ahead to the lobby of a Tire Store.

the poet took a seashell from inside his coat and placed it next to his ear.

he spread his fingers and stuck his thumb to the side of his head so that it looked like antlers or antennae.

stood like that for a moment and took his hand down and put the shell away.

then he continued to explain. people are tired of having their poetry interrupted by cappuccino machines. people want poetry that is interrupted by pneumatic drills. they want compression and rattling of chains. people waiting in Tire Store lobbies want poetry. Even if it just allows them the chance to tell people how much they hated it. even if they act embarrassed for the poet. or become angry and walk out. or throw you out. but they want it. if we had only taken the Poetry Reading immediately to a Tire Store the people in the lobby would have saved it. we wanted to save the Poetry Reading ourselves but we were just a bunch of poets and the best we could do was sit with it. hold its hand and watch it breathe its last.

ok? said the poet.

SO WHAT I GOT TO LAY DOWN ON YOU

Kats and Kitties this evening is this-

If you got that spring in your step, joy in the hearts and a smile on your faces...there are terrible things about to befall you. You know it's true. Now w/attitudes like mine and ideas like mine about politics life and Religion. I have constantly got somebody trying to turn me on to their brand of nationalism, spirituality, or else they want to check out my chakras w/some kind of crystals or somethin' like that.

One woman in particular told me she could prove, God exists. So I pulled up a chair. She said, well, just take a look on out the window there...

so I looked on the window expecting to see divine beings dancing, Saints blowing trumpets and rays of sunlite pouring out of the heavens like liquid-

gold. But all I seen was rocks and trees. I said-all I see is rocks and trees. She said, That is the Father's Creation. No mother involved, said I-you Got it wrong if there's not a woman involved then it's not creation it's masturbation. After that she left me alone. Which is what I had wanted.

Your ambitions will always be getting tangled up w/your convictions. Making it hard to let your hair down or up as the case may be.

Up on the building. Working w/Ned there. I am scared. I sure do hope we don't fall off-I say. Oh-he says-I'm not worried, I'm ready to leave this sinful wicked world any day and go on up to, Glory be w/the Lord. Well, I decided I was gonna test this man's convictions that were obviously Tangled up w/his ambitions.

So I grabbed Ned by the back of his jacket and acted like I was gonna throw him off. You know what? Old Ned fought like crazy to keep himself from

being thrown off that rooftop and so I told him-You see there Ned you

ain't ready to go to glory today. And wild-eyed Ned left me alone for a long

time, which is what I wanted.

Another day, another man. Come into work rantin' about singing and dancin'

And romancin' on television. Why me and my boys can't hardly watch an

Afternoon of car racing w/out some half-naked woman trying to sell us

a case of beer- Well I can solve your problem-I said. He wanted to know

how-I said-My TV is broke why don't you bring your TV over to my house

and you and your family won't have to look at none o' that sin. Of course

he kept his TV, they always do.

Because a person's ambitions are always getting tangled up w/their convictions.

And making it hard for them to let their hair down or up as the case may be.

Ned says he's been married fifteen years-and never seen his wife naked.

I said Ned how'd you get two kids? He said we do it proper we do it in the dark.

Knowing Ned and Bernice—I can kind of understand that one. Still-

Your ambitions are going to get tangled up w/your convictions and make it hard

For you to let your hair down or up. As the case may be.

But if you ain't got no spring in your step. No joy in your heart. And can't

Find a smile to put on that pretty face…

Some blessings are about to be bestowed.

THE OLD BULL

This is the day that the Lord has made.

And this is the shade that the green tree gave.

This is the grass where the old bull grazed.

And this is the ground where the body was laid.

Oh even in the spring everything is dying.

And I'm just a man that the Lord hath made

Out of dust and spit and lust and rage.

And I've been shipwrecked from truth.

And I've been shipwrecked from beauty.

And I've been shipwrecked from love.

But mostly I've been a witness to brutality.

The universe is expanding; it will collapse someday.

Turning back the page,

We will come back and make the same mistakes.

Infinite mistakes, icing on the cake for your birthday:

Adam, Atlas, Osiris, Jesus.

This is the day that the Lord hath made.

This is the shade that the green tree gave.

This is the grass where the old bull grazed.

And this is the ground where the body was laid.

Oh even in the spring everything is dying.

And I'm just a man that the Lord has made

Out of dust and spit and lust and rage.

And I need a chariot with wheels of fire.

All I got today is another nail in my tire.

I can barely lift my big old Minotaur head.

With holes of fire for eyes.

Mouth full of fangs.

Sucking everything dry my claws can find.

My big old horrible head.

Scarred, wicked, old and barred,

Crowned with horns, eyes full of nothing but dark.

Mouth full of nothing but lies.

Sucking dry everything my claws can find.

I am the ape that speaks.

The child that waits upon the father's wrath.

The Minotaur.

I am a baby in a boat upon a river.

I am building a tower right up to heaven.

Because I wanna see my Daddy.

I haven't seen him in a long time.

And I think he might be up there in the sky.

OHHHH Daddy!

I don't care if he punishes me

As long as he sees me.

Lets me know I'm alive.

God sent his son to die for you.

Sent his son to die for me.

I'm no angel. Angels have wings

Come from living on high

Feeling no pain. Me, I lose my

Car keys and I forget my name.

And I know pain just like a brother.

Dirty old man, trying to drill a peep hole

In the universe. Dirty old man

Trying to see what he can.

Every Adam, dirty old man

Trying to drill a peep hole in the universe.

Using and begging, demanding and accepting,

Down on my knees up on my throne.

Always drilling my dirty peep hole, man.

Dirty old man, hands full of nothing.

Eyes full of everything.

Hands full of everything my claws can bring.

I am an ape.

I am an angel.

I am a slave and a king.

A moron and a genius.

A prophet and a fool.

I am a man.

And there is no end

To the evil that I will do.

ABOUT THE AUTHOR

Ted Pope is a writer, musician, artist, and filmmaker from Morganton, NC. He is the author of *rEd lipstick* from New Native Press and is the featured artist in *Far From the Centers of Ambition* from Lenoir-Rhyne University and Lorimer Press. He was the lead singer and songwriter for Sister Raven and is widely known for his dramatic and often provocative performances.

www.ingramcontent.com/pod-product-compliance
Lightning Source LLC
Chambersburg PA
CBHW031219090426
42736CB00009B/983